A SINGLE MOTHERS GUIDE TO BUILDING A BUSINESS IN 30 DAYS

DEDICATION

I dedicate this information to my children who put up with me and my movements and love me regardless.

To my family

My mother Jimmie Goree

My Father Rufus Goree

Sister Darnita Gainey (Boyce)

You light up my life and you are my biggest cheerleader I don't know what I would do without you sister!

My nephew Jimmy Thomas

My children's father Demetrius Shephard

And his family for being loving and supportive

Daphne D Williams

The person who helped me pushed this babe out and gave me the motivation to get it done in a timely fashion. I love you for just being who you are and helping me even though we have never meet face to face. Yes it is possible to support a stranger. She is my sister in action. I love you for what you have brought to my life.

Tamyara Brown

My sensai! In every sense of the word. Your help has brought it all full circle for me never did I imagine I would be an author of any kind. Thank you!

Kandi KCBIZBOSS Conda

The celebrities in my life on speed dial. I can now call friend. I love being a part of your network and all the great sincere advice you give me daily or when you are not on a plane. It amazes me how you get it all done and still have time for little ole me.

WWW.NATACHAGOREE.PAYCATIONONLINE.COM

WWW.NATACHATAGZ.COM

I AM A BRAND AMBASSADOR FOR KANDI KCBIZBOSS
CONDA (hall of famer)

Once you have formulated your business it doesn't hurt to have a mentor. Someone who gets it and can guide you into your next step.

Meet My mentor Kandi Conda, google her she is AWESOME!! I am proud and pleased to be a brand ambassador for her brand, as well as a friend. Shes pretty much stuck with me for life!

Words become worlds because the universe is always listening!

-Natacha Goree

WE LIVE BUFFALO.
WE BELIEVE BUFFALO.
WE ARE BUFFALO

I LOVE THE CITY I LIVE IN AND THE PEOPLE IN IT DESPITE THE FIGHT TO GET US TO WORK TOGETHER, IT IS AN AWESOME SITE WHEN WE DO COME TOGETHER.

THANK YOU TO ALL OF MY SUPPORTERS AND NON SUPPORTERS ALL OF YOU ARE NECESSARY IN MY LIFE!

REMEMBER

If you get it give it and if you learn it teach it!

I have a story just like everyone else. I am a single mother of 2 teenage boys with a lot of expenses. I also have a loving and supportive family. However I am the only business owner in my immediate family, with a business that is actually feeding my family and paying the bills. They don't understand but they know I'm working and it works. So I will tell you to keep pursuing your vision and never let anyone and I do mean anyone, tell you it cannot be done, there are so many avenues know with the internet and pay pal. There is literally no excuse for it not coming to pass and actually bringing you an extra stream of income. Stay focused and keep fighting. I believe in you even if no one else does. Because trust me you will need to believe in yourself more than anyone else. They all will doubt your ability, show them and more importantly yourself that you can and will do it.

Love and abundant blessings

Natacha Goree (CEO/ Author)

WWW.NATACHAGOREEANDCOMPANY.NET

Table ofContents

Introduction

I am a single mother of 2 teenage boys. I understand what it is like to have 2 incomes in the home and than to have only one. I understand not having enough for food and toiletries. Life can be a wavering ship, however we can steer it the way we want. God wants us to be prosperous on earth. Everyone has a different path to it. The reality is that there is no reality, No one way to get things done. No perfect way to execute an idea. I have had several businesses before actually stepping into my purpose. A lot of fails and just plain one, I gave up on this thing kind of deal, So I get it. You have tons of ideas and want to know how to monetize on them. I get it completely, I live it daily.

I have created some step-by-step procedures in order to get it going for you and help you prepare for the journey. Know First, I would like to let you know I do not have any legal background whatsoever, I am a researcher and love to figure things out. I do not claim to be an expert in anything; however, I do have an LLC with 5 flourishing DBA's. I take short cuts but not with legalities. If you purchased this book it is because you are full of life and need some direction. I am here to help you with that. So without further doubts, lets create another stream of income so you can fire your boss and become what you have been expecting.

These are simple steps to simply help you put what you may already know which can help take you to the next level. Know it is much generalized to prevent from being bias to any industry, but cover all aspects of business.

Make sure you talk to your children concerning this so that they understand what is happening, there will be many changes to mommies schedule and the way you do things around the house normally will change as well. They will notice as children notice everything even if they do not speak up about it. So make sure you are sharing your journey with your children and explain to them the reasons why.

Write The Vision(s) and Make It As Planned

(Lets formulate)

"You can't accomplish anything worthwhile if you inhibit yourself. If life teaches you nothing else, know this for sure: When you get the chance GO FOR IT! – Oprah Winfrey

What drives you to keep pushing? We all have that one thing that moves our soul and we live, breath and eat every day. That is the thing that helps you become a great mom and give 100% plus to your children. That one the thing that you can monetize on. There is another mom somewhere dying to know what you know. And how you make it all work on your own.

TAKE THE FIRST STEPS!

Write it down in a book the moment you have used it and it made you feel great because you know have more time for yourself or your children. Write down the step by step process it took for you to make it or create it. I have some journal space within this book to help you formulate as you go along and turn your dream into income.

KNOW WHAT IT WILL COST YOU!

Even though you will be able to accomplish a little free, you will spend some money to complete your dream. Look into other businesses with similarities as yours and what it took for them to get their own done.

You must know the cost. How much does it cost to make it and how much it cost for you to distribute it? How fast it can be made? Turnaround times are very important to a customer. It also should be important to you as well. You should always clock your own hours.

Write it all down from the kind of car you want to have to the house to the companion and repeat it to yourself daily. This will help you keep a focus on your ultimate goal which you will place in a space that is always in your visual space daily.

PUT IT ALL IN A PLAN (BUSINESS PLAN)
(WWW.BPLAN.COM)

Google business plan template and look at some that have been done before so you can familiarize yourself with the information you will need for a business plan.

Be sure to write a business plan. It is important to see your business on paper and what it will bring to the table for you and your children. How much profit you expect and how much money you will spend if any during the building of your dream.

Do as much as you can for free.Remember googl is your friend.

EIN numbers are free! (Employee identification Number www.irs.gov)

Websites are free! (wix.com, wordpress.com, aboutme.com)

Email is free! (gmail, aol, yahoo, hotmail)

Networking is free! (Webinars, groups on Facebook, some local mixers)

As a mom, reducing cost was very important to me. I am not a cheap skate by any means and I wanted to get the best for my company. So everything I have is upgradable. Yes make sure no matter how you start or what you do. You have nowhere to go.

NOTE SPACE

Time For Some Action

Ok know it's time to put some work in. Create a name for your business. It must be something catchy desirable to say and easy to pronounce. You may want to write a few of them down and mention it to strangers to see how they like it. Maybe present it to a face book group for feedback.

Once you have a name for your business you should Google (www.google.com) it or use whatever search engine you like, but make sure that you search the World Wide Web for it. See if it is being used. Run it through some domain making sites for instance (godaddy.com) and see if anyone has registered the name for a domain. Check book listings see if anyone has written a book about what it is you want to sell or leave your mark on the world with. If nothing comes up then go ahead and grab you a DBA (Doing Business As) or LLC (Limited Liability Company), if you are the creator of something make sure you look into copyright and trademark ownership as well as patenting your idea. Purchase you a domain name for your business even if you do not have a website. I'll explain that to you more in the pages to come. In the mean time lest protect the name of your lovely creation.

DON'T FORGET ABOUT UNCLE SAM

UNCLE SAM MATTERS!

Next, if you are selling items right away make sure you retrieve a sales tax id number if your state has a sales tax. No IRS trouble before you even get started.

EIN numbers are free from the IRS. If you plan to have employees right away or if you want to help, your business(s) have a credit line also register for DUNs number (www.dnb.com). Both will help you in the end. It also depends on where you are as a start up or where you plan to go with your business. That is for you to decide when it is necessary.

(www.copywright.com)

(www.google.com)

Once a name is protected and locked in. start thinking about how you want to present it to the world. Yes, I say the world, because family and friends is not your client. Maybe at some point they will be.

GET SOCIAL AND PUT IT OUT THERE! BUILD YOUR BRAND!

You can start with social media, anything from chat pages to live stream. Either way make sure that you sign up for something to get people familiar with your product and or idea. Just as long as you let the internet knows that you exist. (Twitter, Facebook, Pintrest)

Make sure you create an email address for your business. Even if you don't have a domain, Email contact is going to be a big part of keeping clients and networking with other business owners.

Let your children help you create your product or go on post office runs. Make sure they are involved in every step and the processes that you have created.

MORE NOTE SPACE

Keep Putting In Effort

Know that you have built you a shell its time to get other things formulated like open a Bank account or pay pal to star (www.paypal.com), for your business. Even if you just put 50.00 in the account to keep it open. Open a simple account with minimal transaction fees. Something where you can let the money sit for a long time without penalty. Remember you are a start up with children. Paypal is always great there is no deposit requirement and you can connect it to a business account when you open on at the right time if need be.

Create or purchase some kind of budgeting system to keep track of all money coming in and out and for what reason. There a lot of them out there so use what is user friendly for you not what other people are using because it is popular. At the end of the day it is your books and the IRS is going to ask you about them, not the person who suggested you use that system or your tax preparer.

A short list of a few: QuickBooks, Capterra, Sage, Just to name a few.

Retrieve your business a DUNS number. As you start selling and putting yourself out there you want to build credit for your business. This is the way to do it. Just like a social security number for your personal credit. The DUNS number is the social security number to your business. Because truthfully it will help you more than harm you to have it. (www.dnb.com/duns-number.html)

You may want to register or join some small business groups in your area. To have other business to connect with and grow and learn from. In addition, gain ideas on how you want to formulate your own business, by the way other people do business; remember none of us knows it all, we just know many different ways.

www.sba.com

(small business association)

A mentor is never a bad idea. Churches have bishops, Schools have teachers, and Children have mothers. So you have someone that you can call on for help with your business. Find you someone that is like minded and has the same interest in seeing you grow and become the best CEO you can be. Someone that can be there for you when you when you are breaking down. Will never tell you to quit, or get a job or abandon ship.

Don't Give Up

There will always be someone telling what you cannot accomplish your goals, from family to friends to everyone. You must not only motivate yourself daily but sometimes hourly. Make sure you take time to spend with your children. Formulate a schedule for yourself. Have a timeframe for what you are going to do and when you will finish it. Time is so precious in business building. You have to be wise about it at every moment, especially if you are working a 9-5 and building. It can be difficult to do both. You will need to make sacrifices for your goals. You will also need to cut back friends that take up time that can be used to build that goal. The mindset change is real. No different than going on a diet or starting to workout. You will make decisions on what is more beneficial for you, to hang out or get your budget done? Only you can answer that for yourself. You have purpose and goals, the only way to get them done is to stay laser focused and work at them daily. If you have multiple ideas and ventures such as myself, Write them all down pick the ones that you can accomplish right away first then execute the plan daily until complete and move to the next venture.

Make sure you keep some daily motivation in your life, whether it be music, words of encouragement, prayers. Something that you helps daily to you keep peace and love flowing. You must create such a positive force around you that negativity doesn't even get a response.

LET'S GET A DOMAIN NAME!

Now grabbing domains is a major move. It can even become an extra stream of income. I purchase domains for every idea I get. Sometimes people buy them from me. Now I am no lawyer nor do I want to tell you how to run anything. I am simply providing other mothers with information that people will have you in long drawn out webinars or conference calls and charge you crazy prices to tell you. As a single mother I have no problem investing in myself and making sacrifices for my businesses to flourish. However, a lot of the information people are paying for is free! EIN numbers are free, websites are free, marketing can be free as well and so much more. There is no excuse not to flourish in business within the first 30 days of launching your idea or product as long as you stay dedicated and laser focused.

Keep a pen and paper with you at all times from ideas and impromptu bump info's. The opportunity may present itself in the most unexpected places. Stay ready!

www.godaddy.com

(register domain names)

Invest In Yourself, Your Brand and Your Business

Ok so you have done as much as you can for free mom, now it is time to invest in yourself. If you have do not have a passport, now is the time. You want to have the ability to travel if called upon with no excuse.

If you do not save already you may want to begin to do so, by putting a small amount away either weekly bi weekly or monthly.

Invest in a background check on yourself. People will look into you once you have a business search yourself first before they do. If you find something try to clear it up as quickly and low cost as possible. Invest in a lawyer. Someone who has been doing it for 10 years or longer. Lawyers with that experience will know judges and bailiffs. Which is all in your favor.

You may not have employees at this point but if you do look into creating a SEPA. Which is a 401k for small business owners. It's a way to create a retirement funds for your employees. How great is it that you can retire people from your business.

www.fidelity.com

Stay in positivity as much as possible, and create some me time in your schedule to keep your sanity. As a mother we have the responsibility to take care of everyone but ourselves. Make sure that you are eating healthy and staying active.

NOTE SPACE

The Blessing

The hard part is over. Now you just need to believe yourself. Your business is registered properly and ready to go. Now you need to tell people. Spread the word of your service perhaps give away some freebies or previews of what you are offering discounts or even giveaways and continue to share and network. And then repeat over and over and over and over.

Meet people; boast about your business and product whenever you get the chance. Repeat it so much other people will repeat before you get the chance to.

Last but not the least, always remember the search bar on YouTube is your friend. You can find a training video for anything on there. If you can think it there is someone showing you how to get there on YouTube. Its school and training for small business owners. Save videos to watch later on.

Links, Links and More Links

PROTECT YOUR NAME / IDEA/BUSINESS

www.irs.gov (EIN numbers are free!)

www.copyright.gov (copyright)

www.uspto.gov (patent)

www.godaddy.com (domain)

www.paypal.com (payment system)

www.googlewallet.com (payment system)

www.vistaprint.com (business cards and more service)

www.branbuilderz.com (web design and videographer)

www.adsense.com (payment system for Google and YouTube)

SOCIAL MEDIA MARKETING

www.fiverr.com (hired help for low cost)

www.facebook.com (social Media)

www.twitter.com (social media)

www.pintrest.com (social media)

www.snapchat.com (social media)

www.googleplus.com (social media)

www.amazon.com (seller site)

www.etsy.com (seller site)

www.periscope.com (social media love stream)

www.blab.com (conference visual and live streaming all in one)

www.eztexting.com (text blasting service)

BE CREATIVE (to create flyers/posters for free!)

www.postermywall.com (posters and flyers)

www.picmonkey.com (create collages and posters)

www.canva.com (create posters and flyers)

TIME SAVERS

(Schedule post to your social media and control your email)

www.mailchimp.com (email blasting)

www.unrollme.com (email blasting)

www.hootsuite.com (social media management)

www.crowdfire.com (social media management)

www.freeconfrencecall.com (social media management)

SELF – SUFFICENT SEO

People really do not understand that hash tags are seriously important. Please take the time to do your own research on them and realize they are important to your traffic.

www.twoog.com (register your hashtag, its free!)

www.advertisingwebservice.com (marketing help)

Get Organized

Downloads

Google Docs (to share information and plans easily)

Zoom (for face time meetings)

Use the journal pages in this book to track progress and things that you may have done already.

Always keep some type of visual that can help you keep track of progress and what is left to do daily. Also please never forget to celebrate every single win. It helps to remind you why you are doing all of this. Even if it's something small like a little dance, to having something sweet, or a Manicure or pedicure. Whatever it is you truly love to do. It will help you appreciate your journey that much more.

www.ingramcontent.com/pod-product-compliance
Lightning Source LLC
Chambersburg PA
CBHW070228210526
45169CB00023B/1499